Life's Best Le
I Learned Through *Dance*:
Memoire of a Ballroom Dancer

Lekha Keister

CONTENTS

INTRODUCTION

Why is dance the focus of my memoire? What is so special about professional-amateur dance competitions that I was and remain drawn to it?

I am a career college professor/administrator who discovered ballroom dancing only at age 50. But I have been at heart a performing artist since my childhood days -- ten years of piano competitions in India, preteens through teens; a classical Indian dancer and Carnatic music singer throughout my childhood; and, after I earned bachelor's and master's degrees in English in America, a teacher of English literature, Shakespeare in particular. So you see, performance is in my blood and so also competitions that have me striving to bring out the best in me and in the students I teach.

Although a career as a dancer never entered my mind during my 20s through 40s – I was too engrossed in tumultuous cultural battles, a failed but thankfully short arranged marriage, and fostering my daughter's artistic prowess – my latent dance interest emerged as God-sent just at the nick of time, upon my daughter's departure to college.

Age 51 may seem rather late to take up competitive dancing -- not necessarily, not for a professional-amateur competitor. Age range of amateurs dancing with professionals can be anywhere from preteen to even the eighties. I was fit, had the passionate interest, and limited encumbrances to pursue the field at full throttle. And so I did.

Through dance I have become whole, living life to the fullest. The artistic threads woven inside me since childhood is shaping the embroidered tapestry of my being. I am finding meaning and purpose through dance while striving to live up to my full potential. Dance is thus the focus of my memoire.

My story is unique in that I was able to win over a grand finalist of Professional International Standard in the Blackpool Dance Festival, Blackpool, UK (generally recognized as the most prestigious competition in the world), the United States Open, and the World Championships as my teacher and professional-amateur (pro-am) dance partner. He remained as my pro-am partner for seven years. The other dance professionals with whom I competed in Smooth, Rhythm, Latin, and Theater Arts are national champions with world titles and/or eminent teachers in their respective areas. I have had the greatest blessing of dancing with them in major competitions in the U.S. and abroad.

Since my 50s, I have progressed through bronze, silver, gold, open gold, and rising star categories. Now, into my 60s, my passion continues.

This memoire unmasks the rigor, discipline, and rich intensity of the dance experience – offering a look behind the glamor and grandeur we see on stage. Its central theme is that passion and deep-set needs are timeless and attainable with persistence and effort. Older adults will relate to the experiences of an author who is one of their own generation, who triumphed over seemingly impossible odds and discovered that age is only a barrier if we make it one.

Potential and current ballroom dancers will gain insights from the experiential knowledge I gathered from the best in the field as well as through independent research. They will also benefit from my sweeping personal look at the professional-amateur competitions in American and International styles and theater arts, as well as popular social dances.

I dedicate this book to my husband Dr. Stephen Delin Keister who has been the "wind behind my wings," supporting me through this project and all my endeavors throughout our marriage. I also dedicate this memoire to my daughter Mallika Lecoeur and my three grandchildren Priya, Deepali, and Arthur.

I thank all my dance teachers, especially Giampiero Giannico and Kostadin Bidjourov, who have made me into the dancer I am. I am also thankful to my sister Vinita Ittoop and my aunt Elizabeth Thangaraj for their support and advice.

RECKONING

I was forty-four when my daughter left for college. Yes, it hit me -- panic, disorientation, the whole bit!

Empty nest syndrome, of course. Did not anticipate the full impact, though. Not easy to stop dead on track after years of investing heart and soul raising our only child with extraordinary potential. Mallika would become the class valedictorian of her high school, an opera singer, lead actress in community theater productions, and first violinist in the state youth symphony – all in her teens. Princeton accepted her, so did Barnard College. She chose Barnard to stay within proximity of Juilliard for voice training while pursuing a baccalaureate at Barnard.

Unsettled and dazed as I was at Mallika's leaving, new considerations emerged as I quietened. My husband Steve and I had steered our daughter's success. Ideals of commitment, discipline, and steely determination that drove Mallika stemmed from our journeys together as a family. Painstaking research and pursuit of perfection were behind her every turn. We helped her chart her course. We were important. I was important.

"Stardom" is what I envisioned for Mallika – perhaps an opera singer, a movie star, a theater actress, a distinguished professor, or a star of a different sort that merged all her potential into one.

Having tasted her success thus far, albeit vicariously, it dawned on me that the ball is now in my court. I want to matter as well. Being mother of an ingenious offspring is gratifying. So also, being a Ph.D., career administrator, and English professor. But I want more. I want something for myself beyond the humdrum of routine work-a-day life. Sure, this is happening midway through my life. But yearnings are not time sensitive.

It felt like a calling at that time to reach out into the wide yonder to discover who and what I could be if I allowed myself to let go, be a dare devil. So dare, I did. Counting on all that sank in me through education and experience to navigate future high stakes, I charted me a journey.

Thinking outside the box, I decided that I had to first step out of my comfort zone into a wider social arena to carve out a special niche of my own. What did I know about entrepreneurship or modern clubs, or leaving an indelible mark on society? Perhaps I knew more than I think I know to break out, I reasoned. After all, I had been a communication expert in marketing and public relations as a college administrator and a professor of English. As a stage mother and promoter of Mallika, I had propelled her into promising heights. So why not use those very skills to be a big player in an expansive arena?

And so I approached the Mountain Lakes Branch of the American Association of University Women close to my Kinnelon home. AAUW, I read, is the nation's leading voice for women and girls. I shared its ideals of promoting equity and education for women and girls through research, education, and advocacy.

Within months of joining the association, I assumed the post of writer/editor/publisher of its monthly newsletter, and in three years, the branch presidency. The highlight of my term was a millennium cultural event I organized with a host of talented community women and their spouses – the first of its kind for the branch, complete with a theatrical play, instrumental ensemble, solo singers, and folk dancing. Energized by its success and with artistic cravings egging me on, I decided, at age 50 no less, to try my hand at dancing.

Taking up ballroom dancing was like stepping into a mythical paradise after hitherto level-headed pursuits. Dance would turn out to be the bridge that joined the inherent and cultivated aspects of my personality into a cohesive whole. Dance would intertwine a young girl's fine arts upbringing with the mature adult's academic skill set. Through dance I would become the sum of all my parts, a single trajectory where all previous paths converge.

No question. The circuitous journey I tread was well worth it.

Why so? Let me draw a parallel with Gladys Glover, the star of the 1954 American romantic comedy film *It Happened to You.*

A naive young woman named Gladys Glover yearns for fame. Strolling through Central Park in NYC, she meets a young man, Pete, an amateur documentary film maker who is taking shots of people in the park including the young lady. Gladys who has been in the City for two years, has

just lost a job as a model of girdles because her hip size is larger than it should be. But she still

has $1,000 that she saved up. She tell the young man, "I'd give my right arm to see myself in

the movies. Pete encourages her to follow her dream: "Where there's a will there's a way, and

where there's a way there is a will." They part as friends.

Wandering despondently, Gladys is drawn to a billboard overlooking Columbus Circle with the

notice "Space for Rent." She fantasizes about her name being on the billboard.

The plot thickens as Gladys manages to rent the sign from a busy businessman conducting a

telephone conversation. When the man demands to know whom she represents, Gladys

pretends to be offended: "I'm really too busy for this sort of thing." The spunky Gladys pulls

$1000 in cash from her purse, complains that the man is too "stuck up" to listen to her, asks

"What sort of place treats people that way," and starts to leave. The representative relents and

tells her the sign is $210 per month, three months minimum. Gladys pays $630 in cash and

arranges to have her name put on the billboard.

Within a few days the sign is up. Gladys is thrilled. It turns out that a soap company had

traditionally booked the sign and is upset that another client has obtained it.

The story unfolds with Gladys securing a lucrative deal with the soap executive Adam to give up

her sign in exchange for six huge signs in New York, in lights no less, each saying simply "Gladys

Glover."

Charmed by Gladys, Adam hires her to run a series of advertisements for Adam Soap. But when he later tries to exploit and seduce her, she fights back.

When Gladys returns to her flat, she finds a 16 mm movie projector in her room with a note from Pete the filmmaker telling her to run it. The film plays complete with titles and synchronized sound, entitled "Goodbye Gladys." The charmingly self-deprecating Pete confesses he loves Gladys, acknowledges that his profile is not as good looking as Adams', and says goodbye.

Gladys's advertising career continues, but she finds its emptiness more and more frustrating. She recalls Pete's frequent questions as to why she wants to be above the crowd instead of being happy as part of the crowd. Gladys and Pete eventually get together and plan for their future.

How does this story relate to my circumstances? Well, like Gladys, I am a dreamer. Gladys was a daredevil of sorts when she banked all her savings into becoming famous. She used ingenious ways to stretch the limits of her finances and capabilities to secure her dream. She threw caution to the wind.

Although the film is no more than a comedy about making a fantasy happen, it speaks to real-life possibilities that are within range where there is steely determination and ingenuity to carry ideas forward.

Like Gladys, I seek to fulfill the dream of being above the crowd (but not quite so literally) instead of being just part of it. The film suggests that Gladys secured her dream, with all the pitfalls that came along, and then went on to be happy without any further adventures.

At age 50, my fantasy journey into the world of ballroom dancing has just begun. Now, well into my 60s, I have not come to any juncture to change my course. Unlike Gladys, I see my path forward as a series of adventures branching and burgeoning out in new forms.

There is no ending to this story of a late-start dancer, only new beginnings. Traversing through hurdles and disappointments are part of the course. Knowing that I am gathering knowledge, living fully, and expressing myself intensely through this art form is most gratifying.

The future promise of reaching the pinnacle of my capabilities would indeed be a dream come true. But at the end of the day, what matters is that I have allowed my passion to go beyond practicality to becoming an end in itself.

CIRCUITOUS PATH

April 11, 2020. U.S. has the largest confirmed cases of COVD 19 at 524,576 and 20,254 dead.

NYC, epicenter of the pandemic, is nearing its apex: 87,725 confirmed cases, 5,280 dead. My

home state New Jersey with 9 million people has the second-most cases among U.S. states

after New York at 58,151 confirmed cases and 2,183 dead.

Living under a national state of emergency. Much of the country is in lock down. Sobering

reality to wake up to. Surreal stillness blankets the air!

Time for reflection and coming to an understanding of what all this means. I see a parallel

between living through potent pathogens and overpowering circumstantial events in human

life; resulting changes are bound to be transformational.

Focus herein is on key circumstantial events that shaped my destiny for the first quarter

century -- happenings that sent me on a circuitous journey, first in India, and then in the U.S. I

would emerge as a product of two cultures at the culmination of these powerful developments,

yet uniquely independent of each.

Particularly agitating periods of my life:

- the tremulous two years (ages 10-12) in boarding school after the death of my dear

   maternal grandfather, with loss and abandonment precipitated by my parents setting

   off to the U.S. on a professional tour;

- well into my teens -- the shock of being caught between cultures in a new continent

   upon arrival in America; and most profoundly, perhaps,

- the impact of my arranged marriage to a total stranger and near death from the abusive

   marriage; and also

- separation from my child (left with my parents) to pursue doctoral studies and rebuild

   my life.

Childhood to my mid-twenties were undoubtedly transformational. Despite rude awakenings, I would emerge from these critical years with my intrinsic nature intact. The dreamer that I was (and still am) would rescue my spirit and revive my artistic qualities (my saving grace). A look back to these impressionable years explains who I was and what I would become.

From early on, I had the makings of a rebel seeking to carve out my own space. School was ornery, teachers tyrannical, and drudgery of repetitive work were reasons to fake illness from time to time. Welcome relief came in the form of artistic pursuits.

Fortunately, I come from a family that promoted cultural refinement through the arts, particularly for young girls. When I showed little promise in academics, family members (all of whom now have Ph.Ds.), were not overly concerned. As my mother would say about my sister and me, they will turn out alright in the end. Much more pressure was put on my two older brothers to succeed in academics and sports.

From the tender age of 4, music and dance were my haven. Evening and weekends at home were special when it was time for Carnatic Music lessons. The magical drone of the tambura which I strummed and the melodious harmonium our teacher played would be accompaniments for our young voices – my sister's and mine. On special occasions, we also had a percussionist who played the mridangam and my mother who played the veena.

Learning the Bharatanatyam, starting age five, was more challenging. My sister and I were part of a group of young dancers in a local studio that instilled in us discipline and rigor. We learned the mythology, the traditions, and fundamental values of the art form in addition to steps and technique. The teachers were serious about producing quality dancers.

I plunged into the artistic ventures with dogged tenacity. I remember how exhilarating it felt to perform on stage on festive occasions. Artistic achievements were a redemption when performance in the traditional school subjects was merely passable. I gloried at the applause, the accolades, the sense of fulfilment.

At age five, I discovered piano. The convent school I attended had a joint program with Trinity College of Music, London for piano competitions. Needless to say, I wanted in.

For ten ensuing years, I pursued piano, winning honors and distinction. At age twelve, I gained

the coveted prize of a gold medal for junior level competition.

Dreams of glory abounded when I was recognized at the school as a star piano player. That was

the start of my daunting aspiration -- to become a concert pianist performing at world stages

to thunderous applause.

Rock and roll bounced into the scene about that time. Radio Ceylon's daily broadcast of

popular BBC hits had us - girls within my social groups (including the YWCA, Children's Club,

Rotary Club) - swinging, trying to imitate the twist, the jive, and the Cha Cha. Parties were

abuzz with the rollicking music of the Beetles, Elvis Presley, Ricky Nelson, Cliff Richard, Paul

Anka. Grown-ups were also drawn to Western music, but they largely preferred the sublime

Jim Reeves, Nat King Cole, Pat Boone, Andy Williams, Connie Francis and the great western

symphonies.

As young teens, my entourage of girl-friends formed a band, complete with the Spanish and

Hawaiian guitars, ukulele, the bongos, and the maracas. My sister and I were the lead singers.

Although mere amateurs, we hit the local scene with much gusto. At annual school events, I

was picked as lead dancer for the Highland Fling, Irish jig, and the Japanese Fan dance. So there

you have it – budding of my compulsion for the performing arts.

When my parents immigrated to the U.S. and took my siblings and me with them, the sky was the limit for this aspiring artist. The bubble burst, however, when it became clear in my undergraduate years as a music major that I was not cut out to be a concert pianist.

So English Literature became my passion – the poets of the Romantic Age in particular, and then Shakespeare, Milton, and ultimately the great novelists -- American, English, and the world.

My love for the literary arts actually goes back to age 14 when, inspired by the *Golden Treasury* of poems we used to read in school and a growing fascination for nature, most especially the countless stars of the Trivandrum sky, I wrote a poem entitled "The Fathomless Sky" (got published in the school magazine). To quote a few lines from that poem:

Away in that dazzling celestial height

The queen of the night awaits my rise

And upon my head her light shall alight

To proclaim me sole monarch of the skies

And there in the midst of my heart's delight,

The planets, the stars, and comets that fly

On the silvery carpet of clouds I shall glide

A shooting star to escort me by….

Celestial bodies, the moon in particular, were my fancy then. A short story I published a year before this poem was about a trip to the moon and my encounter there with a giant bird-like creature. Much like Dorothy in *Wizard of Oz*, I was very much caught up in this dream -- scary and thrilling at the same time.

Idealism blossomed as I majored in the Romantic age and crafted my senior honors thesis on William Wordsworth. In graduate school, Milton's *Paradise Lost* and Shakespearean plays in particular captivated by musings. I found Shakespeare to be the quintessential artist, capturing in his characters every shade of the human personality. I was drawn especially to his female characters. I empathized with the fragile Ophelia and the vulnerable Desdemona but was especially charmed by the smart, witty, bold, and seemingly avant-garde Portia, Beatrice, Cleopatra, and even the wicked Lady Macbeth.

Teaching English language and literature was my next natural outlet. Enjoyed it when undergraduates applauded or thanked me for whisking them into far-away lands and cultures through Herman Hesse's *Siddhartha*, and for engaging them in the profundity of Shakespeare's *King Lear* and *Merchant of Venice*.

Within a few years, however, I became weary of teaching the same subjects and so my wanderings drifted to journalism. Happened rather suddenly when an opportunity arose for me to try out for an internship with the *Providence Journal* in Rhode Island. At age 25, I was selected.

In the thick of this new adventure as staff reporter -- interesting part was a police beat on domestic abuse and an unsolved murder, and later, feature articles I bylined on subjects like agoraphobia for the Sunday magazine edition -- I was called back home.   My life was having to take yet another direction.

Arranged marriage was in the horizon. How would a person acculturated into Western society balance two distinct worlds that had come to define her personality to pick the next trajectory? For answer, let me start by going back in time to the values and traditions under which I grew up as a young girl in Trivandrum, the capital city of the South Indian state of Kerala.

Trivandrum, with its undulating terrain of low coastal hills and verdant paddy fields was dubbed by Mahatma Gandhi as the "Evergreen City of India." I was raised amidst the splendor of its ancient palaces, sculptured temples and mosques, ornate museums, beaches nestled by swaying limber coconut trees, and sublime backwaters, lush with palm trees and pandanus shrubs growing alongside.

Built on seven hills by the sea shore and located on the west coast of India near the southern tip of mainland India, Trivandrum is bounded by the Laccadive Sea to its west and the Western

Ghats to its east. The city heralds diversity of religions, languages, dialects, traditions, and customs.

As the state capital, this largest city in the deep south, is an academic and research hub and the state's Information Technology hub. It is home to the University of Kerala and the regional headquarters of Indira Gandhi National Open University and many other schools and colleges. It includes research centers such as the National Institute for Interdisciplinary Science and Technology, and the Thumba Equatorial Rocket Launching Station, later renamed Vikram Sarabhai Space Center (VSSC), on the outskirts of the city.

India's first space rocket was developed and launched from the VSSC in 1963. Worth mentioning that my late mother, physicist Dr. Aleyamma George, was a colleague of Dr. Vikram Sarabhai, internationally regarded as the father of India's space program. VSSC funded her key research projects while in Trivandrum.

The City has traditions dating back to 1000 BC. It is believed that the ships of King Solomon landed in the city in 1036 BC. The city was the trading post of spices, sandalwood, and ivory.

The city's golden age - the mid-19th to early 20th Century - saw the establishment of Sanskrit College (1824), the first English school (1834), the Observatory (1837), the General Hospital (1839), University College (1866), Women's College (1864), The Oriental Research Institute and

Manuscript Library (1909), The first Mental Hospital (1870), Law College (1875), and the Ayurveda College (1889). Engineering college was founded in 1939.

Incidentally, my late mother served as professor of physics at Women's College, University College, and the Engineering College during her tenure in Trivandrum and prior to her departure to the U.S. My father likewise was Dean of Law for the Kerala university system while serving simultaneously as the Principal of the Trivandrum Law College.

With my maternal grandfather serving as the state's high court judge and my parents as academics, my siblings and I were immersed from the very start in the world of formal disciplinary studies. Paradoxically, however, my parents were also steeped in age-old traditions and value systems passed on through the generations. My mother, especially, I would categorize as a maverick in matters of education and a traditionalist in every other sense.

On the one hand, my mother was the first woman in Kerala University to gain a Ph.D. in Physics. On the other hand, as was the usual practice in our Orthodox Syrian Christian community, she entered into arranged marriage with my father at age 19. She was one of very few women in Trivandrum who raised four children while at the same time pursued higher studies -- baccalaureate to doctoral – after her marriage. In the 1960's, she left Trivandrum to pursue post-doctoral studies at NYU for two years. My father joined her the second year when he went to attend a world conference at NYC.

The four of us children grew up in a largely extended family with grandparents, aunts, uncles, cousins, and other relatives living within close proximity. With ayahs to attend to our needs as well as a host of other servants – cook, gardener, driver, and peons that came in and out frequently, our house was a hub bub of activity all day long.

When my mother left for the U.S. the first time, my sister and I were pre-teens. My brother Abraham was already a captain in the National Defense Academy in Khadakwasla (Poona, Maharashtra) and Bijoy, the oldest was teaching in the engineering college. My sister and I were largely cared for by our household staff and my maternal grandfather and his wife (my mother's stepmother; my grandmother had died young, before I was born) living nearby. Although we missed our mother terribly, we had the comfort of our extended family and friends. My father, although busy, made sure that our needs were attended to and that we were engaged in a bunch of extracurricular activities – swimming and horseback riding included.

Many of the values I gained growing up came from a strictly disciplinary setup in a reputed private all girls convent school my sister and I attended. My school mates came from a diverse array of religious and ethnic backgrounds – Hindus, Christians, Muslims, Jews included. There were day scholars and boarders among us.

Aside from traditional subjects, Catholics were required to take catechism classes, and non-Catholics (other Christians included), moral instruction classes. The school inculcated in us a code of ethics, generally regarded by the community of parents as proper standards for young girls. These precepts and social-status-based strictures stemming from parental authority would leave indelible marks.

In my early teens, particularly, I tried to dutifully follow many of the standards, albeit grudgingly, being a rebel at heart. I tried to be demure, gentle, soft spoken, and obedient – lauded virtues for a young girl. It was not considered polite to be overly inquisitive and assertive as a girl child, especially if it meant questioning adult rules.

Outwardly in public, I must have appeared sufficiently feminine since the convent nuns referred to me, approvingly, as the quiet one compared to the naughty little sister of mine who was always getting into scrapes with other kids, disobeying teachers, playing tricks, attracting the attention of boys from the neighboring St. Joseph School (very much frowned upon by our parents based on a strict Indian system of keeping girls and boys separate) and being generally rambunctious.

Unlike my sister who acted out and got into trouble as a result, my rebellion was not readily evident in the public eye, but deep and unquenchable nonetheless, latent and ready to surge when triggered.

When our parents left for America the first time, leaving my sister and me in a virtual nunnery of a Catholic boarding school, my rebellious instinct started to surface. Faced with loneliness and a general sense of desolation in the absence of parents, family, or even friends during

school holidays, I developed a steely determination to fight my way out of the confines of

forced piety and isolationism. My rebellious instincts directed my mind to visions of romantic

love outside the traditional system of arranged marriages. I would find a boyfriend on my own

– a knight in shining armor .

When our family eventually migrated to America in my late teens, my sister and I had to make a

promise to our parents that we would abide by Indian values by keeping the male sex at bay by

never dating. We would stay chaste till our parents arranged a suitable marriage for us. My

parents counted on the fact that our strict upbringing in the Indian convent school had

solidified our moral principles and Christian values.

I harbored a dream of finding a boyfriend, nonetheless. What is the harm in that I reasoned?

Just getting a taste of love in the western sense before becoming bound by practical

considerations.

You see, I did not think that "love" in the western sense was going to be anything more than a

fleeting fancy. After all, it was dinned into me through Indian family traditions, that the

western form of love was like leaping into the air blindfolded. What assurance would there be

that the boy is worthy? In India, a potential groom's background was thoroughly investigated.

Family members far and wide get into the process of determining if the boy is of good repute, comes from a distinguished set of families, and has the potential to be successful. A doctor or a

medical student or an engineer fit the bill.

So those were the guidelines my family followed. They searched high and low for the ideal

Syrian Christian Malayalee boy in India and in America. If the boy they picked was domiciled in

India, the idea was that he would join me in America after marrying me. I was then a U.S.

citizen.

Having already gone through numerous inconsequential episodes of surreptitious love

entanglements since I turned nineteen, and since I did not have anybody in particular that I

wanted to seriously consider for marriage at the time, I gave the idea of an arranged marriage

serious thought.

Chain of events that thwarted the romantic in me: Possible suitors among college students

were barred from dating my sister and me. When we defied family and dated anyway, the

battle forces that family leveled against us were too strong to withstand and suitors were

disheartened or intimidated.

At age 25, therefore, after numerous battles I had waged on the romantic front, I simply gave

up. Reminded incessantly about the values of our age-old arranged marriage system – how my

parents and all our relatives were thus married into well-to-do reputable families and how

there were hardly any divorces among them – I let my guard down. Match making happened more frequently than I can imagine, and ultimately, I simply went along with my parents' final choice of husband.

Although my marriage would turn out to be a mistake, I was blessed with a child. Leaving my daughter temporarily with my parents, I would start a new journey to rebuild my life. But that is a story all on its own in my next chapter.

GORGE TO HILLTOP

"A nose dive," a "clueless plunge into the abyss" are epithets that rightly capture how I went into arranged marriage at age 25. I had no real sense of what I was getting into. This is not to poke holes at a system that has worked for most traditional Indians for generations. Simply, it was not designed for my evolving westernized independent nature. Furthermore, there was an unexpected crinkle that doomed the marriage from the start.

The saving grace that saw me through this unfortunate period was my tenacity and hidden strength that I mustered. I liken this fortitude I possessed to one of Ralph Waldo Emerson's sayings: "The greatest glory in living lies not in never falling, but in rising every time you fall." Going forward after the wreck, my resilient rebellious spirit would grow more and more independent, taking calculated risks to chart a bold course for future fulfilment.

In an emotional sense, I was closer to being a teen in my 20s, blissfully innocent about matters of the heart, tenaciously holding on to blind faith, and forcing myself to entertain nothing but great expectations. I was going to be admired, loved, and cherished. I was even going to write a feature article for the *Providence Journal* about my ideal marriage, complete with pictures.

As you may have seen in Indian movies, I was a bride in royal splendor, draped in an extensively layered gold and royal red Kanjivaram silk sari, decked with pure gold bangles and jhumka earrings, and with freshly picked stringed jasmine flowers encircling my hair bun. Complete with sheer makeup and glamorous eye-do to brighten my face, it was as if I was in a cloud as I walked up to the altar, thinking nothing especially, except that I felt like a princess out of a fairy tale.

How naïve and innocent! All the bookish knowledge I had gathered through non-stop academic and career pursuits, ages 18-25, and trailing off from the beaten path of pre-set traditional Indian norms from time to time did not prepare me for what was to come.

An idealist to the core, I actually made myself believe at age 25 that arranged marriage was the means to fulfillment. Although it seemed somewhat outlandish, come to think of it, I bought into the idea of love budding and blossoming after marriage. After all, I was reared and tethered to the concept through a very sheltered life style from which I strayed at my peril. The reputation of my family members were at stake not only in India but also within the strictly traditional diaspora of Syrian Christians in the U.S., if I even dated, which as you know I did surreptitiously.

With virtually no deep love entanglements to serve as knowledgeable experience, I took the proverbial leap of blind faith. On hindsight, I should have considered that my partner would not necessarily share my cherished ideal of freedom of the spirit. I actually believed that as a couple my future partner and I would learn to respect, love, and promote each other's aspirations. After all, he was supposedly from a distinguished and enlightened family of educationists, top level government officials, and medical professionals.

The brief meeting I had with the prospective groom, a formality prior to engagement, was rather unreal, to say the least. I did not particularly go for his looks, although many thought him handsome. His voice was deep and somewhat brash and lacking in tenderness, I thought, and his manner, awkward. I did not connect. But it would be of bad taste to come this far in arrangements to let such matters disturb the state of affairs, I reasoned.

How can I make a swift judgement of him by a single meeting? I must see what my family sees in him – a tall, distinguished looking, strong-built, God-fearing boy. I remember my father mentioning his ambition to be a cardiologist (he had his medical degree from Kasturba Medical College in Manipal) and how much he loved his family, especially his mother who had passed away. I had met his sister at the initial meeting with the family and we got along well. So I reasoned that the boy would turn out to be the ideal I was seeking.

Suffice it to say, the marriage was in the rocks from the very start. The boy was deeply troubled with psychiatric issues, I would find out. Although he was brilliant academically, he had no self-control over passions that wrecked him. How did my parents and others who endorsed him not know that he was a psychopath?

Apparently, he had lived by himself while attending Manipal Medical College and he had few peers that my family knew. During his early years, he had lived with his parents who were educationists in Nigeria. Accounts of his background, all laudatory, came largely from secondary sources.

After a heart-breaking two years, during which I conceived my daughter, the marriage ended, but not without huge ramifications. My rebellious spirit tried and tried to discover an essential goodness in my partner that I thought I could influence and build upon. But the more I tried, the more belligerent he became, resorting to mental and physical abuse that left me at death's door – I survived after fainting from suffocation.

It was not necessarily courage but a survival instinct that led me to escape the bondage. I had my 6-month old daughter to consider. Fortunately, my distraught parents came to the rescue.

Horrified as they were, they did their utmost to rehabilitate me. Encouraged by my mother, I took to writing a diary of all that transpired in the marriage to help me come to terms. I found solace through books and painful reverie and eventually gained physical and mental fortitude. Six months later, I would leave the comfort of my parents to go on a journey to rebuild my life for my daughter Mallika and me. My toddler would remain with her grand-parents until I was ready to take her with me.

I distinctly remember the parting from my daughter the first time. Armed with resolution to pursue doctoral studies in higher education at SUNY Buffalo, I boarded the plane from Virginia Beach, fully aware that I was embarking into a field of study that was hitherto not in my radar.

Practical considerations: with a masters in English literature, years of teaching experience, journalistic prowess, and research capabilities, I can make the transition into an interdisciplinary field that essentially combines these skills. Yes, I had little knowledge of the nuances of the American higher education system. But that should be easy to overcome with hard work and dedicated study. My aunt, Elizabeth Thangaraj, who was at the time pursuing her doctorate in education administration at SUNY Buffalo was largely responsible for guiding my choice of institution and field of study.

Watching my little one in my mother's arms as my parents waved their goodbyes that pivotal day of departure was excruciatingly difficult. I remember drinking wine in the plane, not a habit of mine, just to get knocked out as panic and claustrophobia set in.

The four ensuing years tested my emotional strength and cognitive abilities. Initial courses I took would see me swerving from lack of adequate background in the field. I was among seasoned professionals -- historians, business and technical professionals, librarians -- who had already made inroads into administration in their respective jobs. Like them, my goal was to eventually carve a niche as a top-level university administrator -- a director or dean. Administration, I decided, was the means to earn a lucrative living that would make me and my daughter self-sufficient. It was also something reachable, I reasoned, since I was already an academician.

It took a gigantic effort to stay on course the first year. Separation from my daughter was the most difficult to bear. Spending most of my study hours in the library, I tried to catch up on the history, politics, organization, and governance of U.S. higher education and comparative higher education (the system in other nations). But sadly, I paled in comparison to my colleagues. Except in comparative higher education where I earned an "A," I barely made B's in other subjects. At the end of the first year, I would receive a letter from the Higher Education department of SUNY Buffalo that I might want to rethink my decision to continue in the program.

After the initial shock of the setback, I decided that I was not going to give up. The first summer back home in Virginia Beach with Mallika and my parents was all about gearing up to tackle four sets of candidacy exams to gain eligibility for continued doctoral studies in the program.

And then it happened. I passed four all-day written exams, one of them --- Educational Psychology – with high distinction. It is this second year that I would meet my life time partner, my soul mate Stephen Delin Keister, who had just joined the program.

Steve is as much an idealist as I am, with hypersensitivity and a vulnerability that I found very charming. Similar to me, he was carrying a heavy baggage – mental crisis emanating from bitter childhood experiences.

Physical and mental abuse from Steve's father, starting from his tender years, was just the tip of iceberg. His parents drank and smoked heavily. His father was engaged in numerous extra marital affairs and his mother would develop paranoia. When Steve's older sister married at the end of her baccalaureate years, in part to get away from a dis-functional and abusive family, Steve was on his own in the middle of the fray. Ultimately, after his parents divorced, Steve would need medical intervention to help him rejuvenate.

Steve found refuge in studies and sports. As an undergraduate at Syracuse University, he won the coveted Newcomen Award for Material History. With a rheumatologist as father (MD from Duke University), a distinguished district attorney as his grandfather, and a line of dignitaries in his family history (General John J. Pershing was Steve's great grand uncle), he was of a venerable stock.

As a teenager, Steve championed in tennis and racket ball. But his prime assets were his avid reading and interest in intellectual matters, his scholarly writings, and his analytical abilities. Needless to say, he was the star in the higher education program, respected and admired by colleagues and faculty alike.

You might say that Steve and I, although from opposite corners of the world, were cut of the same cloth. His vulnerable sensitivities and loneliness matched my predicament. I credit my success in the higher education program to his kind support at the start which developed into a full academic and emotional synthesis, and of course, love. Steve and I propelled each other through the program. We survived on graduate assistantship money (we had no job),

managing meagerly as a couple all through the four years, to come out on top with Ph.Ds. in

higher education.

Incidentally, Steve and I got married at the end of my third year in Buffalo. We did not let the

fact that we were just students living on stipends deter us. The future after the program will be

promising, we decided. After Steve and I married, Mallika would join us in Buffalo and our life

as a family unit would start.

Life after our doctorate degrees was anything but easy. After a year of scrambling around for

suitable jobs, I changed career track to work as a research associate on currency exchanges and

financial news for my brother Abraham's international finance software company,

Multinational Computer Models (MCM) in Montclair, NJ. Steve was able to stay within higher

education, however, getting a job as Assistant to the President of Essex County College (ECC) in

Newark, NJ from where he would go on to hold a similar post at Bard College in Upstate New

York and ultimately rejoin ECC as Dean of Institutional Research and Planning.

Yes, career wise, we were relatively on solid footing in the two decades that followed. I would

get back to higher education after two years at MCM -- first as Assistant to the VP for Academic

Affairs at Hudson County College (Jersey City, NJ), then Academic Affairs Coordinator at the

University of Medicine and Dentistry of NJ (Newark), then Middle State Association of Colleges and University Coordinator at William Paterson University (Wayne, NJ) and ultimately, as Associate Director of Marketing and Publications at ECC.

Our three-member family also had the added benefits of having close family and relatives nearby. My parents lived with my brother Abraham (Ph.D. in International Finance, NYU), married with two children, in Boonton, NJ after they had retired as college professors; my sister Vinita (Ph.D. in econometrics from Columbia University), married with two children was in Jersey City, NJ; and my brother Bijoy (computer scientist) married with two children was in Randolph, NJ.

Although Mallika was our only child, she had brothers and sisters in her cousins with whom she was close. I in turn was able to resume my bond with my aunt Elizabeth Thangaraj from SUNY Buffalo (pet name Leelie -- mother's first cousin from Lahore, Pakistan) who had by then relocated to Leonardo, Monmouth County, NJ (husband Arun Thangaraj [first cousin of tennis legend Vijay Amritraj], worked in Bell Labs while Leelie worked as an administrator in CUNY). My cousin Mariam, pet name Lali, (Ph.D. in Economics; economist at Shell Oil) was also close by. My confidants included my sisters-in-law Mariam George (Abraham's wife and a CPA) and Nidhi George (Bijoy's first wife; he later divorced and married Angelica Faria, composer and former professor of Federal University of Rio de Janeiro, who would also become my confidant).

Yes, times were promising at last. Steve and I had gotten off the ravines to a hilltop, with our daughter and our pet cat Susy to bless our days. I felt safe, loved, and protected in this cocoon, ready to venture out into the world of performing arts again through my vivacious and gifted daughter.

SPIRITUAL AFFIRMATION

April 11, 2020. The day before Easter has arrived in a time of global anxiety. For Christians, the last 40 days of Lent leading up to the celebration of Jesus's resurrection on Easter Sunday is a penitential season of prayers, fasting, and remembrance. It is a special time for Jews as well – recollection and hope with Passover. And for Muslims, the upcoming Ramadan (April 23- May 23), is the holiest time of year for spiritual rejuvenation with a heightened focus on devotion.

What special meaning does this COVID 19 pandemic impart when it is happening during major religious seasons? Or should we not read into this any special spiritual message?

Let me speak for myself. I am not a church-going person tethered to the norms and traditions of the Syrian Christians community into which I was born. But I am a spiritualist. With my early years spent in India, a melting pot of religious and ethnic diversities, I have come to revere age-old philosophies underlying religions such as Hinduism and Buddhism. More specifically, I believe in a universal force, God if you will, and the principle that we can, if we choose, connect with this eternal force through prayers, meditation, and a disciplinary code of ethics.

During the Lent period especially, I follow some of the rituals of fasting and reverie. I try to listen to the yearnings and whispers of my soul and remember the loved ones I have lost.

This year, in the wake of the pandemic, I sense a need to be even more perceptive -- that the universe is signaling portentous transformative changes for consideration. I must regroup, I feel -- i.e., focus attention on things of true value that matter -- moral courage, love, empathy for others ' suffering -- and recognize my own vulnerabilities and strengths

It is time, I sense, to delve into world happenings more deeply and take a decisive stance against perceived wrongs that we humans do to each other -- greed, hate, selfishness, and pettiness, among others, that disunites us as a people.

In our current locked down mode, I have taken to the internet and media outlets to decipher and analyze. Through social media, I speak out with passionate intensity and discuss with all whom I reach about how and why we must make a difference. I petition congressmen, senators, and political and social organizations about instituting policy and procedural changes for the betterment of the vulnerable and economically deprived. I see this pandemic as, hopefully, albeit paradoxically, bringing us together as a people to share, commiserate, and at best, to unify to a larger vision.

I trace the beginnings of my current state of mind to an earlier time when spiritual considerations took on an urgency. I recall how, at age 50, I took stock of challenges and blessings of the past and came to a conclusion that there is meaning and purpose behind why things happened the way they did — that destiny had a hand in it, that I must instinctively trust it to direct me.

My daughter, when I turned 50, was well set for baccalaureate studies at Barnard. My administrative career was going smoothly. My four years of service at AAUW-Mountain Lakes had culminated with gaining the coveted position of president of the branch. The millennium cultural event I had organized for the AAUW was a success – winning me all the accolades I could want. And yet, it was not enough. A deep-set craving surfaced to explore latent unrealized artistic dreams.

What if I could dive beyond the familiar and practical into a fantasy world ? I dared to think. My age was farthest from my mind. I was young in body, lithe, attractive, and bursting with energy. Dance arose as a possibility.

I have it in me, I thought to myself, remembering the dance escapades of my childhood days. What was there to lose? So much living to be had! Flamingo dancing, I thought, remembering the vibrantly wild and carefree gypsy dances I did as a child in flamboyant colorful costumes. I pictured myself as the great Teresa Champion, atop a table, stamping with ferocious intensity. Unfortunately, no flamingo dance studios in New Jersey.

Ballroom dancing was my next choice, although I had no visions of glory when I embarked on it. I would need a partner to pursue the interest seriously and my husband Steve shared neither the affinity nor the fascination.

So group lessons it was, where ladies like me alternated with guys without partners. Turned out that I outshone others. Steeped in this new-found glory, I jumped in when my teacher suggested taking private lessons to prepare for dance competitions. I learned that I could have my teacher as my partner for competitions, otherwise called Professional-Amateur or Pro-Am dance competitions.

All it took was the first dance competition. I was in love with the art, the majesty of the grand ballroom, and the glamor and artistry of the dancers. Stepping into my exquisitely designed classic ballgown, after hair and makeup enhancements, it was as if I had become a fairy tale princess. No wonder that I danced that first time with regal splendor, my body and mind swirling with new energy, releasing endorphins with each move.

The added blessings from dancing: I was worrying less, sleeping better, less irritable at work, at home, and with family, and I felt refreshingly young in spirit -- rejuvenated!

In for the long haul, I advanced rapidly. Rhythm dances at first: the American style rhumba, cha cha, samba, salsa, mambo, east coast swing, west coast swing, bolero, hustle. American Smooth ballroom dances were next: waltz, tango, foxtrot, Viennese. Progressing from Bronze to Silver levels, I competed in regional and national competitions. Although top level placement was rather infrequent in the early stages, I was not deterred.

An ardent competitive dancer, eager to test the limits of my capabilities, I delved deep into the art form, harnessing all the analytical tools I developed over the years. Beyond adhering to disciplinary dictates -- learning steps, routine, technical details, history, artistic precepts – I sought self-discovery through dance.

What was my drive? Conviction and compulsion to listen to my soul!   I aimed to embrace challenges -- not to hold back from fear of failure or societal disapproval that I was on a fool's errand venturing on a craft designed for the young. I was going to create circumstances rather than wait for them. Most of all, I sought to believe in myself wholeheartedly -- not just through the eyes of people who had faith in me, but more importantly, through my own inner being.

The best part is that my life and health have dramatically improved since dance. As George Bernard Shaw put it, "Life is about creating yourself." The process of "creating" can continue for as long as I want.

TRAVERSING THE BALLROOM MAZE

At age 50, I was happily employed as Director of Publications at Essex County College, my first of several posting there. The publications I authored included five president's annual reports, four college catalogs, guide booklet per academic program, and more than 100 monthly newsletters, distributed to donors, alumni, government officials, college presidents, corporations, foundations, and partners of the college. I was also webmaster (or should I say "webmistress"?) for the college website. I won national awards for my contributions and was well respected among my colleagues.

Yes, the creative elements of my job were fulfilling. As time passed, however, the responsibilities were becoming repetitive and so also the marketing and public relations appendages. I was representing an institution, not the capabilities I wanted to manifest as an artist in my own right.

Childhood dreams of becoming a stage artist resurged when I transitioned into Pro-Am ballroom dance competitions at age 51 from diversionary group dancing which began at 50. Having a day job did not rule out the possibility of working toward the ideal. And so I cultivated my dancing skills each and every evening.

World renowned ballet dancer Mikhail Baryshnikov declared, when he delivered the 2013 commencement address at Northwestern University, that the arts inspired him to be a better person. In essence, he described his intense focus, thought, and pursuit of excellence in dance as a process of self-discovery and reaching a greater understanding of the complexities and contradictions of human nature.

Baryshnikov noted, the arts through music, literature, and dance, raises our awareness and understanding of the full spectrum of elements that make us human.

Baryshnikov continued: " ...found that dance, music, and literature is how I made sense of the world…. it pushed me to think of things bigger than life's daily routines … to think beyond what is immediate or convenient."

So I am no Baryshnikov, just an amateur dancer, but striving nonetheless to reach the pinnacle of my capabilities.   Baryshnikov's views resonate in me since I have experienced much of what he has described -- dancing CAN evolve into something more than just physical activity, into an emotional outlet, an intellectual understanding, even a spiritual release.

Dancing is not just stepping to music or for health benefits. Sure, it improves our cardiovascular system, increases our muscle tone, and burns more calories. But just as important, and perhaps more importantly, it can be just what we need to express our core needs as humans – whether it be emotions -- sadness, elation, fury, or rebelliousness -- or a spiritual catharsis. It can be an ideal combination of physical activity, social interaction, and body and mental rejuvenation.

Dance has converged all my previous paths in music and literature into a single powerful, impactful, and meaningful outlet. The art has awakened me from a mundane, passive, routine existence to become conscious, aware, and in every essence, energized and truly human!

So here is my story about the journey – from the time I took up competitive dancing more than a decade and half ago.

To beginners, deciding on what dances to start with and how to go about finding the right teachers and learn about competitions can be confusing, particularly since the world of ballroom dancing is forever evolving and there are multitude of options out there.

I ascribe it to good fortune that the owner of the first dance studio I attended, who became my professional partner in Pro-Am competitions, took a personal interest in my development. My ardent interest and enthusiasm helped, I am sure. He had me competing in twelve American style dances within a three-year period, albeit at introductory levels. This sweeping introduction served me well in later years, helping me accelerate with greater confidence to more rigorous styles and advanced levels.

Before going further with my story let me offer an overview of dance styles in ballroom competitions.

In the US, competitive ballroom dances are classified under two main groups: International Style and American Style. The first is based on standards set by world organizations and the second, specific to the U.S.

A little background on the evolution of ballroom dances: The world's leading board for ballroom dance examination, Imperial Society of Dance Teachers (later called the Imperial Society of Teachers of Dancing or ISTD) was established in 1904. This body, comprised of world class champions and other notables in the dance world, was instrumental in developing dancing styles that formed the basis for international dance standards. Their techniques were further modified and finessed over time by a generation of English and American dancers and dance societies in the 1920s and thereafter.

Today dance competitions, referred to as dancesport, are mainly regulated by the World Dance Council (WDC) and the International Dancesport Federation (IDSF) for world championships.

Countries also have their own national and regional organizations that regulate their own way. The National Dance Council of America, Inc. (NDCA), for example, is the official governing council of dance and dancesport in the USA and the leading authority of dance for professionals, amateurs, and professional/amateur competitors. Similarly in Britain, the British Dance Council grants national and regional championship titles.

Internationally, the Blackpool Dance Festival, hosted annually at Blackpool, England, is considered the most prestigious event in which a dancesport competitor can take part.

International Style dances ("Standard" and "Latin") are judged at this competition and not the national and regional variations of individual countries.

Dance competitions today include amateur-amateur competitions, professional competitions, as well as a relatively new phenomenon that emerged within the last few decades, professional-amateur competitions, otherwise called pro-am competitions. I fall into this very category since I compete as an amateur with professionals as my partners.

As a beginner, ages 51-53, I was first introduced to American style dances -- "Smooth": waltz, tango, viennese, and foxtrot; and "Rhythm": rhumba, cha cha, east coast swing, bolero, west coast swing, hustle, salsa, and mambo.

Learning routines was not my priority during this period. My teacher/partner found that I could follow easily whatever he had me do; not as difficult then since I was in the introductory stages. Having fun was what mattered. Having to memorize routines was tedious, especially with these many dances. So I competed in a laissez-faire manner.

Age 54, I embarked on international style dances. Taught worldwide, "International Standard," commonly referred to as "Standard" dances include: waltz, tango, viennese waltz, slow fox trot, and quick step. "International Latin," abbreviated as "Latin," also includes five dances: rumba, cha cha, samba, pasadoble, and the jive. Both groups of dances are standardized for teaching purposes with a set, internationally established vocabulary, technique, rhythm, and tempo.

Under the tutelage of world-renowned international style dance teachers who were inspirational, my dance life took a turn toward greater intensity and in-depth immersion. Competitions became increasingly challenging as I advanced from silver to closed gold to open gold levels. It required all the efforts I could muster and disciplinary focus to gain mastery of technique, routines, and stylistic nuances.

In light of the fact that Standard dances have become my specialty, let me specify a few unique aspects about the style.

Standard dances are performed by a couple in the "closed hold" position. This means that the couple maintain five specific points of contact for most of the dance. They require a high level of precision and concentration as part of technique. The posture, the hold, and the varied tempo and rhythm of the dances together provide a very elegant look as the couple float across the dance floor.

Central features of the five Standard dances:

1. Waltz

Once called the "slow waltz" or the English Waltz, is danced to about 30 bars or 90 beats per minute. Usually, one step is taken for every beat, or three steps for every measure. Although it is generally slow in tempo, the waltz can have advanced figures that may require six steps per measure, which may be complemented with various turns and poses to make the dance more dynamic.

This is often the first dance performed at Dancesport competitions. Its technique calls for a pendulum swing of the body, parallelism of the feet, sway, contra body motion, and rise and fall.

2. Tango

Standard tango branched away from its original Argentine roots by incorporating European influences. In the Argentine Tango, a dramatic and romantic dance, dancers remain closely interlocked and move with passion and precision.

Standard tango techniques dictate that partners arch their upper bodies away from each other, while maintaining contact at the hip in an offset frame. Argentine Tango moves such as the boleo (swinging a leg into the air) or the gancho (wrapping a leg around the partner's body) are not used in ballroom.

Standard tango is generally danced at about 120 beats per minute and in 4/4 time. Unlike it Argentine counterpart, ballroom Tango requires that steps stay close to the ground. Also staccato movements such as the head snap are specific to ballroom Tango.

3. Viennese Waltz

So-called, to distinguish it from the Waltz and the French Waltz, is the oldest of the modern ballroom dances. It emerged in the second half of the 18th century from the German dance and the Landler in Austria and spread to England in the early 19th century. The course of its development to its current form is also a story about cultural changes throughout Europe.

Originally, the couples did not dance in the closed position as they do today. The hold was at times semi-closed, and at times side by side. By the 1930s, however, it evolved into the first dance to be danced in the closed position.

Danced at about 180 beats per minute, the Viennese Waltz is a rotary dance in which dancers are turning in clockwise and anti-clockwise directions, gliding across the floor in 3/4 time. Initially, the dance consisted only of turns and change steps. Additional steps such as fleckerls, pivots, and underarm turns were incorporated later.

4. Foxtrot

The slow foxtrot is a variation on the quicker One Step or Two Step which was popular in the Victorian era and carried over to the night clubs of New York in the early 1900s. It's a graceful and fluid dance with a pace of around 120 beats per minute in 4/4 time. Weight changes and sway is particularly important in the dance since it relies upon a good deal of back and forth movement.

5. Quick Step

Originating in England in the 1920s, the Quick Step is an energetic dance with a great deal of momentum. This dance shows influences from dances like the One Step, the Charleston, and the Shag. It is done in 2/4 or 4/4 time. While it appears smooth and graceful, the dance often consists of a series of hops, runs and rotations. The Quick Step sequences can last for several bars of music, and couples must be prepared to dance with speed and fluidity across the floor.

Mastering all five dances in light of their differences is quite a challenge as each requires a unique, dynamic, and fresh set of skills. Passion drives me to work hard, keep my physical body intact and my mind strong and resourceful as I stay abreast of competitive demands.

Theater arts ballroom show dances have also become part of my competition repertoire, particularly over the last five years. I get to synthesize the styles I have learned over the years into this creative dance form – complete with drama, improvisation, and communicative expression.

SALSA & SWING AS CROSS-CULTURAL BRIDGES

My dance life has centered around competitions. But that is not to say that I do not enjoy social dancing with friends. Seasonal holidays like Xmas, New Year's Eve, Valentine's Day, St. Patrick's Day, Easter, Halloween are dress up days for fun casual dancing and improvised comic routines. Rhythm dances are especially popular among participants (recreational dancers and competition dancers alike) in dance studios, clubs, and home parties. Celebrants include everyone who has a mind to dance -- young and old caught up in the festivities of the season.

Two popular music and Rhythm dances that I have singled out herein for analysis are noteworthy not only due to their immense popularity in America and abroad but also the potential they hold for bringing us closer as a world community. I refer to (1) Salsa music and dance; and (2) Swing Jazz music and dance. I have traced the evolution of these dances and the powerful impact they have had in the 20th and 21st century.

Salsa

As the name connotes, salsa today is a "spicy sauce" of a musical and dance genre that evolved from many roots. Musically, it encompasses a variety of redefined and reinterpreted Latin Pop music genres, instrumental combinations, and cultural influences ranging from Cuban son Montuno, Puerto Rican bomba and plena, Dominican Merengue, Cuban Yoruba ritual music, and Afro-American jazz and rhythm and blues.

The evolution of salsa to its current rich intensity is a story of fusion of U.S. and world cultures. Its jazz and Cuban connection can be traced back to many jazz artists in the U.S. interacting with Cuban music as far back as the early 1900s. Its Puerto Rican roots and Latin elements in general came from the influence of Latin musicians of South America and the Caribbean who came to the U.S., especially New York City, in the 1930s and 40s. Another important antecedent of salsa is the mambo. The structure of mambo, which is a fusion of "big band" jazz and Afro-Cuban rhythmic organization, has become the basic format for many New York salsa bands.

More recent influences on salsa came during the 1970s through the cultural exchanges between Cuban and Puerto Rican immigrant communities in New York City. The genre developed further through the influence of music and cultures from many parts of the world while its locus was New York City.

Highly danceable, salsa's rhythms are hot, urbane, rhythmically sophisticated, and compelling, bearing unique features of the regions where they are performed.

In New York City where the salsa bands first performed, for instance, the high concentration of Puerto Ricans and NuYoricans (New Yorkers of Puerto Rican descent) has led to the Puerto Rican style of fast flash footwork in salsa. There is also a strong Latin Hustle influence in New York salsa dancing, seemingly a byproduct of the disco craze, which was Huge in the Big Apple in the late 70s and early 80s (as seen in "Saturday Night Fever" when Tony Manero [John

Travolta] is King of the Latin Hustle in the local Brooklyn discos.

In Los Angeles, the dominant influences are from Puerto Rican salsa, Latin ballroom, and lindy hop (an American dance that originated in Harlem, New York City, in the 1920s and 1930s with the jazz music of that time). LA style salsa dancers often develop highly choreographed cartwheels, flip routines, and dips and spins and drops in their movements.

The salsa phenomenon has spread throughout the Americas and to the rest of the world, connecting people of different cultures almost seamlessly. Salsa dance clubs have sprung up in cities as diverse and far from New York and San Juan as Stockholm, Tokyo, Sydney, and Berlin.

It has become so widespread and popular around the world that salsa bands comprised of talented musicians and vocalists who are not Afro-American, Puerto Rican, Cuban or even Latin have emerged across the globe, attesting to the integrative and transformative influences of this fusion genre.

Swing Jazz music and dance

Ken Burns's PBS documentary series, "Jazz;" 24-hour jazz radio stations like WBGO-FM with its non-stop on-line component; award winning apps that offer eclectic current, historic, and international music of jazz masters; and "The Jazz at Lincoln Center" programs in NYC today attest to the widespread popularity that jazz enjoys in contemporary society.

Since its earliest days on the streets of New Orleans, jazz has bridged communities with diverse ethnic, cultural, and social backgrounds, speaking a common musical language that people understand. As delineated below, jazz has crossed national borders and challenged the status quo, and is an example of how an art form contributes to changing social, economic, and class relationships.

The story of jazz began as a story of struggle, particularly in the early years of the genre's conception. The original African American jazz musicians did not readily gain acceptance for the new musical genre they created. An emerging brand of "swing jazz" was the one exception. The special sound of this dance-oriented "big band" created by African American composers like Duke Ellington and Count Basie took America by storm, thanks to a new generation of white musicians and dancers who brought their music to the forefront.

One of the early successes of the genre was the music that Duke Ellington christened "Swing" with his 1932 hit record, "It Don't Mean a Thing If It Ain't Got That Swing." In 1935, white bandleader and clarinetist Benny Goodman purchased the arrangements and led swing jazz to popular mainstream. Goodman would go on to gather an extraordinary group of performers into his high-profile band, including Fletcher Henderson, Gene Krupa, Lionel Hampton, Peggy Lee, and Stan Getz. His decision to integrate his group with black musicians helped begin the slow process of integrating the music industry. Other white swing jazz musicians who brought the genre to it immense popularity were Glen Miller and Artie Shaw.

The evolution of swing jazz is also a story about some of the greatest swing jazz vocalists like Ella Fitzgerald, Frank Sinatra, and Dean Martin, to name just a few.

Swing jazz was characterized by strong rhythmic drive and by an orchestra "call and response" between different sections of the musical ensemble. The rhythm section – piano, bass, drums and guitar – maintained the swinging dance beat, while trumpets, trombones, and woodwinds and later, vocals, were often scored to play together and provide the emotional focus of the piece. This arrangement resulted in a "conversational" style among sections that arrangers exploited to maximum effect.

Mainstream America began to dance to swing bands during the 1940s. Early swing dances like the Charleston that has retained mainstream popularity to this day supplied to America what European dances lacked; it engaged the freedom of full body motion. Swing dances marked a break away from the constraints of post-Victorian morality and disregarded what was graceful or what wasn't.

The attire associated with the swing dances mixed African and European dress norms. European skirts rose to expose more of the calves, and tops shrunk to bare the arms. This runs in contrast with what was acceptable in the European or Judeo-Christian aesthetic in which drawing attention to a woman's sexuality was forbidden.

In the 1930s and 1940s, when railroads were moving people across the nation, shows like the

"Ed Sullivan Show" were moving culture and idea. By the 1950s, teenagers were watching lindy hop on television and trying it out at local-dances.

Hollywood picked up on the swing dance phenomena from the 1930s into the 1950s and created over 100 movies with stars like legendary Fred Astaire, Ginger Rogers, Gene Kelley, Cyd Charisse, and Rita Hayworth that included choreographed swing dancing scenes.

Much of the swing era dances that surfaced evolved from the Afro-American tradition – from the tapping of Bill Robinson and Fred Astaire through the shimmy of Gilda Fray, and social dances such as the Charleston, the lindy (or jitterbug), and the twist. All of them mirror the changing social climate that began questioning established techniques that limited access to non-trained dancers.

But not all Americans were enchanted by the widespread success and influence of swing jazz and the challenges to social norms it represented. For example, although the races were generally kept separate in the early years of swing performances, there were consistent expressions of outrage at the energetic dancing that accompanied concerts and persistent criticism of the influence of swing music on young people. Young white women were especially targeted by those who considered swing "mulatto" music and wanted to preserve a fantasy of white purity on the dance floor and the bandstand. America's conflicted response to the rise of swing and its connection to black culture is clearly articulated in "The Benny Goodman Story," a Hollywood film in 1955 about the swing era.

Yet, jazz would go on to break through cultural barriers throughout the 1940s and 1950s with the emergence of iconic jazz soloists/bandleaders like saxophonist Charlie Parker and trumpeter Dizzie Gillespie. They influenced the development of bebop and modern jazz. The late 1960's would witness the emergence of jazz rock, a musical genre that developed from mixing funk and rhythm and blues rhythms.

The development of more jazz fusions in the 1970s ushered in a new wave of popularity for jazz, ultimately spawning "smooth jazz," a musical form that gained mainstream positioning.

Swing dance styles similarly evolved past the early decades of the swing era and today bear close association to dances such as the hustle, and, as earlier noted, the salsa.

Swing dances continue to climb the respectability ladder. Beyond the night clubs, bars, and social events, they are making their mark as formalized competitive dances within nations and across the globe. We have today, for example, the "American Rhythm" competitions (standards set by USA Dance) that includes east coast swing; the International Latin competitions (standards set by the World DanceSport Federation) that includes the jive; and the competition series of the World Swing Dance Council that includes the west coast swing. Venues for the competitions and the list of participating countries are world-wide.

In sum, swing jazz is here to stay, as attested by the trend of burgeoning fusions of this genre (in music and dance) spreading across the globe. The Xmas holiday season includes such popular programs in New York City as "Diva Jazz Orchestra Celebrates Ella Fitzgerald's Swingin' Christmas" and "Jazz at Lincoln Center Celebrates Big Band Holidays," and similar programs across the globe.

Let it also be noted that the inclusive approach of swing jazz and jazz in general have released musicians and dancers from the restraints of individual cultures to explore new pathways of multiculturalism, which in turn holds promise for greater understanding and integration of the global community.

One such integration happened in December 2015 when an ensemble of young Cuban jazz musicians performed for the first time on American soil at Chicago's Auditorium Theatre; it was just the previous year that the US began restoring diplomatic ties with Cuba, severed a half century ago. The concert was the dream of both Chicago Jazz Philharmonic's Artistic Director Robert Davis and the 24-year old conductor of the ensemble, Ernesto Lima.

"Jazz is improvisation, and improvisation is freedom," said Lima. Davis similarly expressed his own sentiments about the historical musical breakthrough: "The music is everybody's and it's what they value. If they can trust us with that, they'll trust us with other things."

US-Cuba relations have soured since then, but music and dance have a way of surpassing impediments. As is apparent today, politicians come and go but music and dance in all its

evolving forms are here to stay.

DIPS & SPIKES

The transition from recreational carefree dancing to a powerful all-consuming passion was paradoxically a result of what seemed like a disastrous turn of events at the close of my fourth year at the first dance studio.

In the early years of dancing I was in lala land. Expectations were limited to just having fun: first, with friends in group classes and later, with a larger society of competitive dancers. One-on-one performances of show dances and even the more challenging regional and national competitions with my teacher were mainly for thrill, devoid of much anxiety.

Good and carefree times, however, came to a close when studio politics and questionable contractual arrangements ended my commitment to a place that I had come to call my second home.   I could no longer count on the only teachers I had known for four years.

Randomly I sought advice from everybody I knew in the dance world – competition cameramen, videographers, former students of the studio, and friends among competitors to figure out what I should do next to pursue training with leading dance professionals.   Armed with the feedback, I pursued one lead after another.

Joining forces with a male amateur dancer, I would travel to New Brunswick, almost thirty miles away from my home in Kinnelon, to train as a couple with professional Standard dancers Rita and Gary Gekhman, featured artists in the popular television series "Dancing with the Stars." When my partner found this arrangement tedious and after I was involved in a car accident during one of my commutes, the efficacy of this set up became too uncertain.

Next option: working with teachers in two major NJ dance studios -- Starlight Dance Center in Nutley and Paragon in Roselle Park to determine the right fit for my partner and me. Eventually we chose having private lessons with a world-famous dancer at Starlight, both as a couple and individually.

That was the pivotal moment when my dance life turned around to what it is today. During the period, however, my dance partner lost his regular job as a computer scientist and left dance altogether.

I alternated between private lessons with Paragon's star teacher Igor Litvinov, winner of professional Russian National Championships, and Starlight's Giampiero Giannico, grand finalist of Professional International Standard in the Blackpool Dance Festival, Blackpool, UK (generally recognized as the most prestigious competition in the world), the United States Open, and the World Championships.

Some elaboration is warranted on how I managed to win over world class dance teachers Litvinov and Giannico to offer me private lessons and later, to be my professional partners in prestigious professional-amateur nationwide competitions.

The saying "the less you know the better" worked. With virtually no connections with important people in the dance world and with no more than cursory experience in Standard dances (I had focused on American style Smooth and Rhythm dances at the first studio), I expected to convince teachers who worked with seasoned dancers to teach me, a virtual beginner in "Standard."

Suffice it say, my naivete paid dividends. I let my passion take over the delivery of my introductory speech; my fluidity with the English language also helped, I suppose. At the end of the day, each was willing to give me a try on a trial basis. Although I must have been pitiful on the first trial lesson with each of them, I learned that they were intrigued by my enthusiastic spirit. And so it happened that I overtook many others (I later learned) in securing a spot for weekly lessons.

From private lessons in the basics, I progressed to competition level dancing. Initially, my pro-am dance partner in dance competition was Litvinov. Although I had not danced above the bronze level in American style ballroom and never competed in Standard, Litvinov believed that he could get me ready for a national competition – Capital Dancesport in Baltimore, MD – with four months of intensive lessons. And so he did. Furthermore, we competed not in Bronze, but in the Silver level and won that championship.

I continued private classes with Litvinov and Giannico until I had to make a choice between the two over who would be my Pro-Am Competition partner for the long run. I loved them both but I knew deep down that Giannico was the best fit, aside from the fact that he was world renowned and most highly in demand among top amateur women competitors to be their professional partner in competitions.

Although I parted company with Litvinov to choose Giannico, I have great respect for Litvinov to this day. He remains my friend and we are each other's well-wishers.

Transition from American Smooth to International Standard was not the only move I made after I left the first dance studio. With my background in American Rhythm, I embarked on International Latin dancing at Starlight studio under the tutelage of Rising Star World champion Andrew Phillips. This move occurred at relative ease. Phillips had taught at the studio that I had left and was on board with my making this shift.

My most productive years of dancing then ensued. Four Pro-Am national competitions a year in Standard dances and four in Latin. I progressed through Silver to Close Gold in Latin and Standard and continued further to Open Gold level in Standard.

I competed in Latin not only with Phillips but also with British Nationals Professional Latin Champion Paul Richardson and trained also under Richardson's professional partner (later his wife) Olga Rodionova (also British Nationals Professional Latin Champion). Unfortunately, a number of medical problems I had with my knees came in the way of advancing to Open Gold in Latin competitions -- the Jive required intense rapidity of movement that my knees were unable to handle.

While I have departed from Latin dancing and American Smooth over the past few years and from Rhythm dances for over a decade, they have each left a lasting impact – specifically, transferable skills that I integrate into theater arts show dances.

These show dances which have become a part of my repertoire over the last five years, enable me to fuse any number of styles -- standard, smooth, Latin or rhythm-- into a cohesive whole. They enable me to get to the core of a song or character and express truth, as I see it, through emotion, passion, and sensuality – the heart and soul of creative dancing.

I credit my development as a dancer in the last seven years to my current teacher and professional partner in Pro-Am dance competitions, Kostadin Bidjourov, World American Smooth finalist, U.S. Open Professional Theatrical Ballroom Champion, and current member of Fred Astaire Dance Studios' International Dance Council. Bidjourov, a master choreographer of show dances and a stellar designer of ballroom dance costumes, has propelled me to new heights in Theater Arts as well as Standard. Giampiero Giannico also continues to spur my development, coaching Kostadin and me on a regular basis.

A few years ago, I also ventured into the field of Argentine Tango in a bid to learn some of its nuances that I now apply in show dances.

Dance in any form that my body has the ability to master has always intrigued me and driven my impulses. I welcome this sensibility since it makes me feel alive. Pressing my way through internal and external turbulences is well worth it, I believe, when the reward at the other end is personal spiritual fulfilment.

WHAT IT MEANS TO DANCE

Think of a dance you watched that left you with a sense of awe?   Was it the intricacies of the art that moved you or something more -- the way the dancers shared a part of their soul through the medium?

The essence of dance at its best, I have learned over the years is the seamless confluence of the head and the heart. Head is the knowledge base and the heart, emotions and passions that undergird the movements. A dancer who evolves to this ideal stage is soulful -- effectively authentic, intuitive, expressive, grounded, creative, and thereby, moving to audience.

In pursuit of this very ideal, dance has become for me a deep and stimulative experience. But there is another dimension as well. "Shiva," Lord of the Dance in Indian temples, signifies dance of life, a metaphor for the cycles of life, for change, for transformation [as noted by Johannes Beltz, Curator of the 2008 Shiva Nataraja exhibition at the Rietberg Museum in Zurich].

In line with this context, I liken dancing to a "rite of passage" from nearly three decades of largely mundane existence to a higher plain. It is as if all the knowledge, experience, and gifts I have acquired over the years are moving me in a more powerful, transformative direction.

"Dance of life" also symbolizes a process by which we reach and celebrate self-realization. As literary scholar Sherman Paul has noted: "To dance …is to enter into the motions of life. It is an action, a movement, a process …to dance is to know oneself alone and to celebrate it.

Other observations of significance:

Dance is the hidden language of the soul. -- Martha Graham

We dance for laughter, we dance for tears, we dance for madness, we dance for fears, we dance for hopes, we dance for screams, we are the dancers, we create the dreams. -- Albert Einstein.

These holistic perspectives lend credence to the view that dance, both literally and metaphorically, signifies freedom, self-exploration, self-expression, self-discovery, and self-actualization.

Let it also be noted that dance signifies our very entry into this world. Life starts with movement and breath, followed with self-expressive gestures – what dance embodies.

Putting all this together, I regard dance as an attribute of life with many manifestations: as a continuous process of creation, evolution, and transformation; and as a latent pulsating energy of my spirit. I release that spirit when I dare to dream and with confidence, ride the plethora of emotions to freedom -- i.e., I dance metaphorically and literally to find harmony/balance within myself and to soar to higher plains.

Beyond rudimentary levels, I have evolved as a dancer through a stage of passionate outbursts as an energetic Rhythm and Latin dancer, to the ethereal and sublime in Smooth and particularly in Standard. True, ballroom Tango can be fierce and passionate and the Quick Step, bouncing with energy. Still, they have to be executed with delicate intensity and finesse in a synchronous, stable, and contiguous relationship with a partner.

Through ballroom dancing, I have especially learned the lesson of refined intensity. In the beginning, my tendency was to let myself go in wild abandon -- the tendency to collapse or crash into a step without deliberation -- as opposed to being in control over each segment of a movement through precise body positioning and maneuvering.

Learning to control a movement is essential for precise execution -- whether it be in sports or in the arts. While there are unconscious motions in our body that most of us cannot control - such as breathing, heart-beat, functioning of the internal organs - conscious movements can be masterfully controlled through processes to optimize their effectiveness or artistic rendition.

In advanced levels of dance/theater arts, it is especially incumbent on the learner to fine-tune movements to almost an exact science through optimal control of his/her movements.

To maximize the effectiveness of endeavors, here are some basic principles (learned through teachers and independent research) I consider:

Process, precision, and details matter from the very first leg of the journey to the very end.

*Be very clear in your mind on what to do, how to do, and the expected outcome before you proceed into action.

*Demonstrate your poise and determination as you take the first step and keep that strong frame in check throughout.

*Execute each action in precise sequence - what must come first, what follows, etc., as opposed to side-stepping a part of the sequence or just falling into it in a jumbled or erratic manner.

*Remain focused on details as opposed to letting your body deflate/collapse/ lose energetic determination as you move from the beginning to the end of a sequence - i.e., don't pull the plug out of your energetic frame of mind.

*Treat every step - from the beginning to the end - as a fresh start, with the same power, strength, and precision.

*Keep the mind in the forefront of the action through steely determination as opposed to letting the mind drift into a dreamy/passive state with the body moving simply through inertia.

*Finesse the finish of an action instead of collapsing into it.

Cultivating an assertive and independently powerful spirit takes much practice and patience. I have found it helpful to start practicing the precise movements at a slower pace and increase the pace as confidence builds. Eventually, as in every learning experience, the movements become so entrenched into my being that it feels like second nature.

Dr. Ruud Vermeij, dance educationist and psychotherapist, describes this stage as "bringing learned and therefore controlled movements to our unconsciousness." Vermeij explains: "A dancer constantly practices movements with a conscious mind, then allowing the movements to sink into the unconscious mind. The dancer can now execute endless and complex combinations of individual movements with remarkable speed, especially when performed in succession." The caliber of the movements would rest on the quality of the dance practices.

When you display professional ease through your finely tuned actions and creativity, you project a sense of confidence and elicit the public's delight and approbation.

But advanced technical capabilities should be considered as a conveyor rather than an end in itself. I have evolved to realize that a true artist projects meaning or a truth behind the moves.

As Martha Graham notes:

I wanted to find a way to reveal the inner landscape – to chart a graph of the heart.

... the essence of dance is the expression of man – the landscape of his soul. I hope that every dance I do reveals something of myself or some wonderful thing a human can be.

An exquisitely designed sailboat is ready for take-off. From the bow to the sternum, every part is ship shape to work together to move and steer the boat. The day is gorgeous, lots of sun, and a masterful captain is in full gear. But something is missing. No wind -- the heart that drives the boat to its fullest possibilities.

Here is the point. Without meaning behind the steps, without saying anything through movement, without passion, even the most technically brilliant feats of a dancer does not transcend to the highest level – artistry that touches our emotions.

A performing artist with superior technique may be able to defy gravity, spin countless rounds, or have extensions that mimic contortionists. But without emotional content that is part and parcel of artistry, technical prowess may well seem like a "bag of tricks" that mean and convey not much more than athleticism.

Artistry is when a dancer becomes the music, and watching in the audience, your heart catches fire. It's the most precious feeling in the world, like being in love. Sometimes we call it musicality, but it's more than that. It's the wedding of musicality and technique to make meaning. The audience feels the dancer is saying something vital and truthful.

Artistry may also be viewed as analogous to poetry -- free and spontaneous; creativity unfettered by mental deliberation or compulsive controls; simplicity that emanates from intensity; the finesse of all that we have learned that is coming from deep within our soul. One may also encapsulate this ideal in the words of Leonardo da Vinci: *Simplicity is the ultimate sophistication.*

Let me backtrack now, to the journey I have pursued as a competitive dancer to where I have arrived.

When I first entered the competitive dance arena, I was singularly focused on winning. It gave me a feeling of self-worth and a sense of pride to perform better than others. Over time I found, however, that while winning felt good, it was not a lasting sensation. How do I compare with other more accomplished dancers in more rigorous competitions? Not so good, I knew.

A true sense of accomplishment, I recognized, comes not just in winning but in whether or not I optimized my level of capabilities in a contest, or else, shouldn't I be choosing only easy feats that I can effortlessly overcome – nothing to sing about?

The only masterful creation to work with is myself, I realized. As Michelangelo stated, "Every block of stone has a statue inside it and it is the task of the sculptor to discover it." It does not matter what anyone else is doing to liberate their stone; it is their intention. I need to focus on how well I am doing with my own block of stone. And when I persevere, stay focused, stay on course in the wake of setbacks, dig deep, and think beyond the box, I will discover new ways to succeed and may well fully develop my true potential.

Bruce Lee, Hong Kong American martial artist and film actor, has said, "The successful warrior is the average man with laser like focus." I keep this idea in mind especially when pressures of competition build up. Having had my share of past impediments -- disparaging criticisms from others, previous disappointing performances, and fear and anxiety overshadowing physical preparedness – staying focused is easier said than done.

But here are some of the principles behind "focus" [acquired from my teachers and through independent research] that I try to apply. In essence, I must concentrate on staying in charge of my body, my mind, my dance in preparation and during performance.

Physical and mental preparation for dancing must start long before stage performance.

Mental rehearsals or "visualization" of actual performance can enhance psychological, emotional, and technical skills. Visualize what you want your body to do and keep thoughts positive. When you plant an intuitive thought and let the image grow through repeated mental performance, you induce physiological changes and increase accuracy. You are in effect training the relationship between the mind and the muscles.

Dancers who keep a healthy positive conversation going, create within themselves their own motivation and encouragement. This inner dialogue can reduce tension and create ease in movement. Don't let negative thoughts creep back and ruin your technique.

*Have a well-articulated action plan. Research has shown that people are more motivated and work harder when they have clearly defined objectives toward which to work. But it is critical to follow through with the action plan. Quoting French poet Antoine de Saint-Exupéry, my teacher Giampiero Giannico has often said, *"goal without a plan is just a wish."*

*Do not set unrealistically high goals; you will become easily disheartened by lack of progress in attaining them. The key to success is incremental progress through a series of small goals and plans of action. This approach enables dancers to be more narrowly focused on what is important to realize their expectations and full potential. The process will also provide the benefits of self-confidence, motivation, and discipline.

*Goals are not always reached, but if plans are executed consistently, there will be improvement. The effort involved in striving for a goal is as important as reaching it. Personal and artistic growth is from the effort and not the attainment.

*Accomplishing a goal can reinforce the habits and routine and produce a spiraling effect of greater motivation, improved results, and increasingly higher goals.

*Optimal performance is not obtained by being totally relaxed. Moderate anxiety boosts

adrenaline and drives energy to necessary parts of the body, such as the legs, thereby enhancing strength and coordination.

Include progressive relaxation in regular practice to condition the body to effectively use the technique to moderate anxiety levels. Essentially, you tighten and relax four major muscle groups: legs, chest and back, arms and shoulders, face and neck. You would start with the legs and work your way up: three seconds each for tightening and relaxing. Also tighten and relax your whole body, three seconds each. You would use your personal cue words for each such exercise. The objective is to condition your body to the cue words so that each time you get nervous, saying the cue words would in effect get your body to respond accordingly. If tension persists in particular areas, do extra relaxation exercises in that area.

Let your eyes or face express conviction when you dance. They complete the line and the beauty of the musical phrase.

Ultimately, dance requires the ability to concentrate on a variety of changing things at once and an ideal concentration is having a sense of total awareness: of the stage, your proximity to other dancers to dictate adjustments that need to be made, and a proper temporal focus -- on the present, not the past or the future.

Classic example of loss of concentration: doing exceptionally well in the first part of the program but faltering in the second part. Beginning to anticipate the bravos or thinking "I've done it," are in essence telling the body to relax. When the body relaxes, it constrains blood flow and also the necessary flow of adrenaline and oxygen to perform at the peak level.

*Concentration problems can also arise from anticipating performance. Loss of concentration can produce thoughts such a "I've got to concentrate" or "try harder" -- self-induced pressures that increase anxiety levels and which in turn interfere with the body's ability to perform at a high level.

As I progress through advanced dance syllabi and increasingly challenging theatrical routines, the principles of "precision," "artistry" and "focus" I try to follow are bearing fruit. Armed with tools I can use, there is, thankfully, less uncertainty and a greater sense of personal power and mental stability I feel on the competition floor.

I plan to continue to finesse dance the rest of my life. Distilling the art to draw out increasingly clearer essence has become a gratifying, purposeful endeavor.

Finessing is a natural progression for artistic growth. It must be distinguished, however, from strictures that confine the body and soul. Like the butterfly that can get crushed if we hold it too tightly or the grains of sand that can trickle through our fingers if we squeeze our palm tightly to hold on, I may inadvertently stymy my artistic (i.e., creative) capabilities if I try to control artistic outcomes.

So my charge must be to be free to create. Technical expertise, already being ingrained in me (and growing), will come into play as I spread my wings. Freedom, peace, and aliveness can let my inner wisdom and natural sense of ease and love radiate though expressiveness in dance. I am then about to make each moment as a performer vital and worth living.

Sure, I will not be without pain and frustration as I grow as an artist. As Martha Graham has noted, *No artist is pleased. There is no satisfaction whatever at any time. There is only a queer, divine dissatisfaction, a blessed unrest that keeps us marching and makes us more alive than the others…. Dance is the song of the body, either of joy or pain.*

EMOTIONAL TRUTH

Dance, happily, is unfolding my intrinsic qualities like a tree bearing leaves, flowers, and then fruit. I am especially heartened that my innate spontaneity, free spirit, creativity, and love for aesthetics are being realized through dance and an increasingly responsive public. Even as I continue in my struggle to finesse technique and artistry, I feel a growing confidence that my perseverance and love for the art will see me through.

Artistry, the wedding of musicality and technique, is increasingly my focus these days as I dive into the world of solo (albeit, with my partner) theater arts show dances.

Coming from a background in piano, musicality, is ingrained in me; I am able to hear subtleties in a score. Musicality in dance is interpreting the subtleties with my body. With my teacher Kostadin Bidjourov's guidance, I am learning to translate nuances in mood and musical essence by playing with dynamics and timing.

For instance, to express greater intensity or drama, I sometimes hold a developé for an extra moment or find where I can balance longer or fit one more turn into a sequence, as opposed to simply doing sequential steps to music (which makes for a repetitive/boring look). As Wade Robson, choreographer and "So You Think You Can Dance" regular explained to Dance Spirt magazine, "musicality is understanding music on a technical level and then dropping all of that knowledge so you can sit deep inside the music... It's dancing inside the music, as opposed to floating on top of it.

"Dancing inside the music" is also bringing out the emotional truth underlying the composition so that the audience feels the dancer is saying something vital.   Singer and actress Audra McDonald said in a 2015 interview [with the *New Tribune*] that emotional truth is "about getting to the core," to a deeply human essence of a song or character and conveying that intensity of feeling in a meaningful evocative presentation.

The question becomes: does the dancer's message and meaning reverberate with the audience? Is there a heart-felt connection with the audience that arises through the unfolding of a story or the emotions in the music? Has the dancer hit a nerve that is reverberating with the viewers? Is the dancer's performance thus authentic?

The fact of the matter is that meeting such standards requires hard work : research interest, acting ability, and creativity as much as technical prowess.

To express the content in as deep a level as possible, the dancer, together with the choreographer, would have researched the composer's intentions and meaning, the history of the piece, and the nuances of different interpretations to reach his/her own conclusions. My background in English literature, including studies in the enactment of Shakespearean plays, makes this part of the process especially interesting.

Acting and being creative in movement come rather naturally for me, thankfully.   Attuned to the rhythm, melody, and mood of a song, I enjoy translating the musical notes into expressions of my own, i.e., emotional content.

Technical prowess becomes the key to genuine delivery of emotional truth. My goal is to work toward making musicality and technique coexist as one during performance. I would not want to take any short cuts on this matter. Overdramatization, shoddy, or forced movements will be seen by the public for what they are – as fake and artificial. I aim to make performances as authentic as possible -- have my body become the music.

BURDENS AS SOURCE OF STRENGTH

To know what I must do to achieve successful outcomes is not the same as effectively doing them. The human factor – vulnerabilities physical and emotional – has countered many an endeavor. How do I best proceed knowing this possibility? Perhaps the better question is: do vulnerabilities have to dampen my efforts or can they be harnessed to my advantage?

The traditional notion is that vulnerabilities, notably fear and anxiety, make a person weak. For a dancer, it may be argued that "practice makes perfect" does not necessarily apply; that performance jitters and weight of meeting expectations can louse up even the most well prepared.

"More smiling, less worrying…" "Don't worry, be happy…." easier said than done. Emotional duress has a way of creeping up from time to time. Trying to suppress through distractions or pretending to be strong, I find, are unproductive. Escapism and denial only exacerbate the situation since the underlying problem will reemerge regardless, even more forcefully.

A better approach, I have found, is to accept, it's what it is, and come to terms with it. As per Car Jung, "what you resist persists." Conceding that emotional turbulence is just one of those things that can happen to anybody is possibly the key to regaining composure and arriving at a sense of inner peace.

Over a period of time, these situations have become less disturbing when they occur since I have learned to see what American historian Alice Morse Earl has observed, *Every day may not be good... but there is something good in every day.*

Weight of high expectations that I carry at dance competitions are in part due to perfectionistic tendencies. The laudable aspects of my perfectionism -- I tend to be organized, self-disciplined, conscientious, and exacting. But striving for a very high level of performance acumen (seemingly commendable), is not realistic when I have not reached the optimal level of training. I have had to remind myself, "I am not there yet."

Not so laudable side of my perfectionism: tendency to spaz out on getting things just right and ending up with the opposite result. Beating myself up and feeling bad, oftentimes I fail to stop and learn from the experience. Result: coming to a virtual standstill in my development. Fatigued mentally from the process, what an effort It has been to get on up, regain a positive spirit, and work diligently and purposefully.

It took a while for me to develop a true insight and in-depth confidence to accept that I, like everyone, makes mistakes and that mistakes are not enemies that I have to avoid but friends who can propel me to advance each time I learn from them.

Aside from unrealistic expectations, I used to base my worth on public acceptance, recognition, and acknowledgment of what I do. How I was placed in dance competitions was especially critical in the initial years of competition. The times I made it to the finals made me feel admired and loved. But no single successful outcome was enough. Comparing myself with others, I wanted more and more.

It was indeed a maturing process when I stopped judging my worth vis a vis others. I am no more faulty than others who are themselves imperfect by the very fact that they are human, it dawned on me. I further realized that my appeal [when I started to place first in intermediate level theater arts solos] may be not necessarily in how "deft" I am but perhaps in how authentic I appeared with unique and possibly endearing imperfections.

Over time I also realized that while it is laudable to do well in competitions, it is just a short stop in my journey to reach my full potential. That means embracing future challenges with confidence without being deterred by setbacks. It also means enjoying as worthwhile the richness of the process and not just the outcomes.

The ultimate breakthrough would come when I am ready to accept who I really am. As Fanny Brice noted, "Let the world know you as you are, not as you think you should be..."

I have dwelled enough on my emotional vulnerabilities, now to physical burdens I carry.

In my mid thirty's, long before I took up dancing, I was diagnosed as having osteoarthritis of both my knees. The condition was especially painful before dancing, but happily, it improved once I took up dancing, coupled with disciplined exercises and fitness training.

At age 53, however, I had a setback. I needed meniscus surgery for my left knee, and my right knee, although less impaired, had also weakened. The protective cartilage of both my knees had worn down considerably. The damage was irreversible but I can manage the problem so long as I stay fit and be active, I was told.

Within a month after the surgery after a number of physical therapy sessions, I went back to dancing despite swelling now and then around my knees, lack of flexibility, and discomfort.

The situation has vastly improved since those days after I started on an injection routine every six months. I call it a medical miracle -- the injections of the medication called "euflexa." Although the injections by no means alleviate the pain altogether when I go deep down on my knees, I have learned to cope with the difficulty.

In addition to dancing every day, I start off with a daily yoga routine of exercising my upper body, legs, and knees to maximize flexibility and lubricate my joints. Weekly GYROTONIC practice with my personal trainer is also part of my retinue to builds core strength, balance, coordination, and agility. Despite all these measures, I am not without pain when I engage in routines that are hard on the knee. But it is a no brainer. Dance will be with me forever, at least for as long as destiny will let me be.

As a special note: Euflexxa injection contains a synthetic version of synovial fluid found naturally in joint spaces. By injecting Euflexxa into my knees, the viscosity and shock-absorbing properties of the synovial fluid can be restored, reducing joint pain and stiffness.

Today, as I am seated on my sofa, clicking away my story on my laptop computer, with my kitty "Brookie" curled up next to me, I marvel at how far I have come in my dance journey despite obstacles and setbacks along the way.

It is also an uncanny time for me to be writing this story, when COVID 19 has almost the entire nation in lock down, when death and spiraling cases are in the news every day – truly heartbreaking!   I have also been battling a flue (not COVID 19, thankfully, or at least I hope not -- no testing is available) for nearly two months. And before the flue, I sprained the MCL cartilage of my left knee during practice; I recovered in a matter of weeks with physical therapy. The long shot is that I lost considerable weight and feel too weak for dance practice -- hard not to do for close to three months!

Still, there is this one silver lining. I have unleashed my cerebral energy into writing my story – yet again, my weight has become my strength.

AN END IN ITSELF

"Spinderella," is one of my many nicknames that I treasure. My dance teacher, Giampiero

Giannico, coined that special word in jest when he found me adding spins to a carefully

choreographed routine I was supposed to master.

"You have a creative way of covering up your mistake," he laughed. Sure I did. Actually it was

instinctual. It has always been my mode, even as a child, to come up with original ways to

deflect attention.

My childish nature extended to prancing and spinning around the floor as a make-believe

ballerina. I suppose some of that stuck, since the idea of dance stayed with me all through the

years.

So where have I arrived in this journey of mine? Are the outcomes what I envisioned? Where

do I go from here?

Starting with blessings of dance: I feel alive, driven, creative, and ready to take on more

challenges. My energy is disciplined and structured. Dance has sharpened my character,

making me ever more tenacious and determined. I have grown stronger as a competitor thanks

to guiding principles and an ever-growing knowledge and skills base. I have gathered powerful insights from the very best in the field. I feel immensely gratified that I have had the

opportunity to dance on world stages with dance icons. The more I learn, the more humbled I

am about the enormity of the field, the surface of which I have just scratched. Yet I marvel that

destiny has put me on a course for more and more discoveries.

The journey has been anything but easy. I have been characterized as hypersensitive, prone to

emotional volatility and mood swings, and being very hard on myself. My teachers had to have

believed in me to set me on the right path despite my eccentricities. The more difficult lessons

I have learned are to manage defeats, moderate expectations, accept uncertainties as a given,

enjoy the process and mini gains, and value my capabilities instead of looking to others for

affirmation.

I am now starting to see my worthiness as a natural unfolding, as something I can avow, not

something I have to earn. I must continue to trust in this sensibility as per this saying: *A bird

sitting on a tree is never afraid of the branch breaking because her trust is not in the branch but

in her own wings. BELIEVE IN YOURSELF. --- Anonymous*

Entering the sphere of theater arts show dances in the last few years has been especially

rewarding. I now have the chance I have always wanted to creatively depict on stage the

substance of a character or the depth of feeling in a musical piece. In essence, I am exhibiting

my very vulnerabilities – pains, sorrows, traumas I have experienced – through the characters I am portraying. When I draw the sympathy, love, and trust of the public, I feel buoyed. After

all, show dances are designed to pull at the public's heart strings.

In the cabaret show dance "You Don't Own Me," for instance, it has been cathartic to depict

rebelliousness - my own instinctive nature - in the dance. Dancing the "Black Swan" is letting

out the free spirit, lush romanticism, and heart felt poignancy of the bird, again feelings

encased deep within me.

My next show dance will be dancing to Mozart's "Laudate Dominum," a celebration of

greatness in art, an emotionally deep and celestial piece. Incidentally, I will be dancing to my

daughter's pure and angelic rendition of the piece; at age fourteen [1992], she was the chosen

soloist for a select troupe of teenagers [the US Youth Ensemble] and a professional pianist to

perform the piece at the Cathedral of Notre Dame in Paris.

It was the right move to have waited until I had acquired advanced level skills in ballroom

dances before I transitioned to show dances. Knowledge of a myriad of styles (in Rhythm,

Smooth, Standard, and Latin) helps and so also the flexibility, agility, strength, and balance I

have developed over the years. Fusing ideas together is a rewarding creative process.

Going back to when I first took up serious competitive ballroom dancing, I remember the issues raised by family and close friends: Why go into competitions? Why not just enjoy recreational dancing? Isn't it too expensive to compete Pro-Am? What is so important about competing this late in life?

Vincent Van Gogh has said: *What would life be if we had no courage to attempt anything?* My frame of mind at age 53 was exactly that. I have the health, the body, the passion, and the courage for competitive dancing.

Prior to the twentieth century, the thinking was that "death begins at forty" as most people didn't live much beyond that age. Life expectancy in medieval England was around twenty-five years and only reached forty sometime around the turn of the twentieth century. Life expectancy has continued to move up and forty now seems no age at all. In 1991, the *New York Times* printed this opinion:

All our age benchmarks, which used to seem solid as rocks, have turned into shifting sands. Life begins at 40? More like 50.

Opportunity for ballroom dancing and the means did not strike me when I was young. But with my daughter off to college, I had fewer encumbrances to pursue heart-felt artistic needs. Recreational dancing is well and good. But I can do more, I reasoned. The rigor and high standards I must meet to be a competitor should put me on track to discover my true potential. Unlocking my potential may be the key to self-actualization, I imagined.

True, Pro-Am competitions are definitely expensive. The higher the world standing of a professional, the steeper the rate. Salaries my husband and I earned were decent . Nonetheless, competition expenses stretched our limits, particularly when I was competing alongside two world class professionals in Standard and Latin, not to mention the cost of custom-made, ball gowns and associated appurtenances.

Familiar clichés come to mind. "Where there's a will, there's a way," "Opportunities are like sunrises. If you wait too long you miss them." The golden opportunities that came my way: being situated in the New York/New Jersey metropolitan area with the finest caliber of professionals from across the world to learn from; gaining the confidence of a grand finalist in world championships who was willing to be my Pro-Am partner.

So competitive dancing it was. I had no doubts.

As to what I expected to accomplish as a dancer was an evolutionary process. Initially, it was to win over others in competitions. My sense of worth depended on it. Today, however, it is more about how I view myself, irrespective of how I am judged. Winning feels wonderful, of course! But losing is not as devastating as it used to be. I know that there will be many more competitions to do better. So I look to each competition as a chance to execute what I have strenuously mastered, and learn what areas need improvement. Each competition is a stepping stone to more thrilling challenges.

"Reaching out" is what makes my life's journey powerful and meaningful – an end in itself. It is as if I am a bird taking off into the wide yonder with outspread wings and unbridled force. So much to experience and master. I welcome the liberation that sweeps over me when I dance. It is in part a fantasy with no limits. And yet, it can be more than fantasy. It can be real – a lifelong journey to unravel the mystery of my very being! As in Matthew 7.7, *Seek, and ye shall find; knock, and it shall be opened unto you.*

LEGACY

I remember the first time I saw Rodgers and Hammerstein's *My Fair Lady* at the Trivandrum movie theater. I was fifteen at the time. How charmed I was by that high-spirited Cockney flower girl, Eliza Doolittle (actress Audrey Hepburn)! Rebellious as she was, Eliza put up with her benefactor Henry Higgins's (actor Rex Harrison) tyrannical speech-tutoring so as to learn to speak like a "proper" upper class lady. When she first gets her diction exercises right – "The Rain In Spain," she is ecstatic. She sings, "I Could Have Danced All Night."

I could have danced all night

I could have danced all night

And still have begged for more

I could have spread my wings

And done a thousand things

I've never done before

I'll never know what made it so exciting

Why all at once my heart took flight

I only know when he began to dance with me

I could have danced, danced, danced all night.

How the lyrics of the song and buoyancy of her spirit reverberated with me! Eliza was no more than a common flower girl. But when opportunity for social betterment struck, she went for it with all the gusto she could muster. What a rapturous outpouring at her first success!

Eliza's words bring to mind the exhilaration I felt as a first-time competitor in a grand ballroom. Today, I remain excited and determined as ever but there is a difference. My dreams are not just centered around me. I want to make a difference to the people whose lives I touch.

It has been most gratifying, for instance, to learn directly and indirectly that my performances have inspired people to take up dancing or try out challenging styles like Quick Step and theater arts. Teenagers are among the people I apparently inspired, some of whom are now competitors.

Today I enjoy teaching dance at my home town library and also in my home studio. My students are largely older folks from the community who were drawn to dancing after watching *Dancing With the Stars* on television. Their joy of learning to dance is contagious since I am equally inspired by their progress and determination.

The ripple effect of my contributions is wonderful to watch. Every year I have more and more people drawn to dancing. They tell me how much happier and healthier they feel as a result.

While dance continues to be central in my life, I have other wide-ranging interests as you will have noticed, specifically English language and literature. This area of specialty is how I got involved in a unique project, Shanti Bhavan, starting in the late 1990s and continuing to this day.

Shanti Bhavan is a state-of-the-art boarding school for Dalit children (so-called "Untouchables" living in poverty) near Bangalore, India. Serving as a board member of the George Foundation [my brother Abraham George is its founder] that started the school as the Foundation's first project, I take pride in the part I played to get the school established. I produced the school's first operational manual, taught English literature to the seniors, and am still involved in promotional activities.

Shilpa Anthony Raj, among the school's first graduates has published her story, *The Elephant Chaser's Daughter*, which I helped edit. Shilpa is now in the doctoral psychology internship program at Hofstra University.

Shilpa's graduating class of 2010 is featured in an Independent film *Backward Class* that won accolades at the May 2014 HotDoc Film Festival in Toronto. *Daughters of Destiny*, a Netflix film chronicling the life of five young Shanti Bhavan women, won the 2018 prestigious "Television with a Conscience" award by The Television Academy Honors.

The success stories of Shanti Bhavan graduates who hold jobs all across the globe are featured in world media outlets including the BBC, New York Times, PBS, ABC World News, the Wall Street Journal, and Times of India. It is a source of great joy that the children of Shanti Bhavan have flowered so bountifully!

In closing, let me just say that life's lessons have been immeasurably rewarding. I share my experiences as a way of letting readers know that being an artist can be both challenging and exciting at the same time. How much of our heart, mind, and soul we put into our efforts make all the difference.

PICTORIAL HISTORY

1960 – Lekha and Vinita (sister), Trivandrum, Kerala, India

1968 – Lekha as Gypsy Dancer, Trivandrum, Kerala, India

2002 -- Lekha and Brian Nash, Nash Dance Center, Randolph, NJ

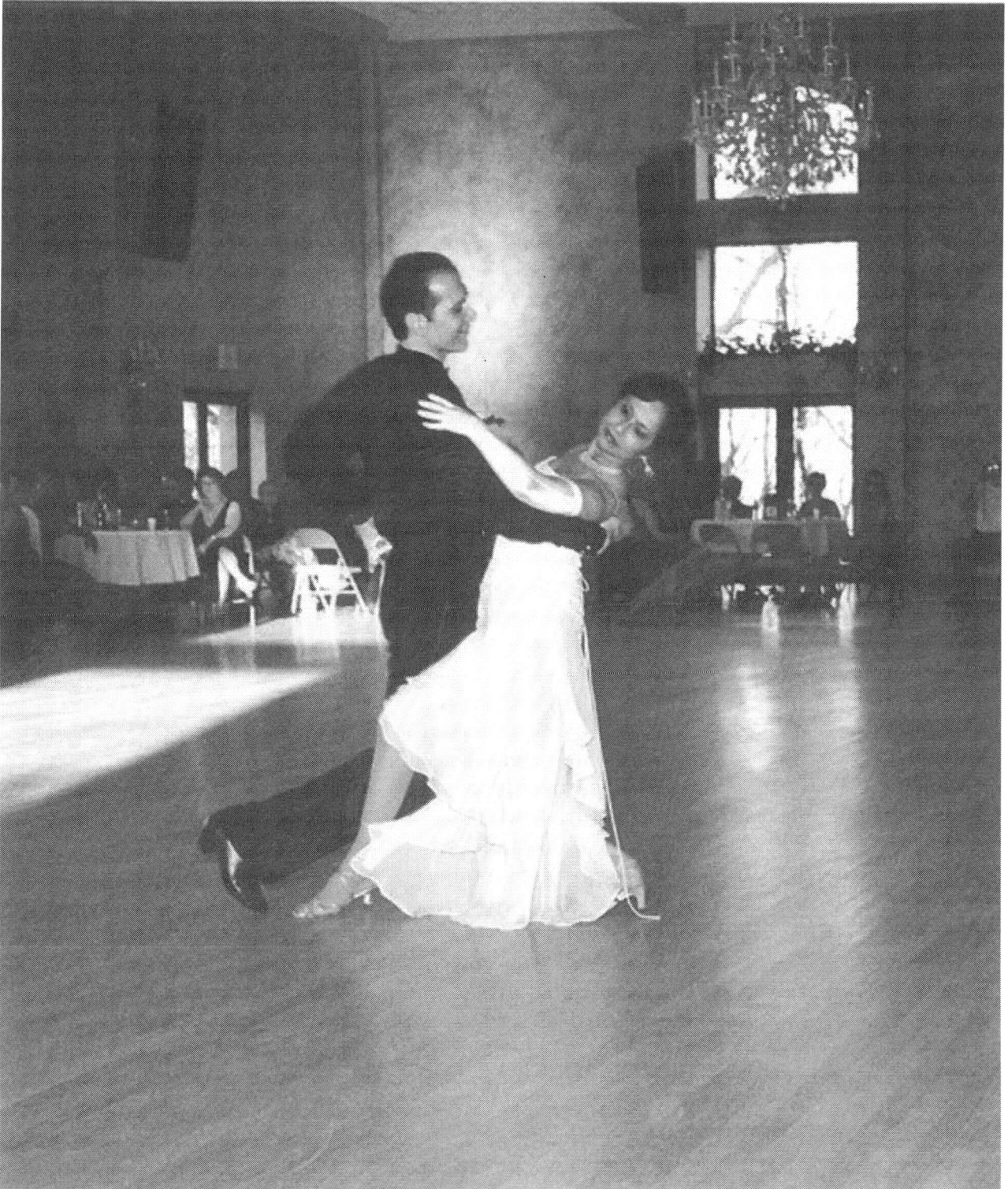

2005 -- Lekha & Ian Folker, Showdance, Nash Dance Center, Randolph, NJ

2006 – Lekha & Andrew Phillips, Ohio Dancesport Championships, Columbus, OH

2009 – Lekha & Igor Litvinov, Capital Dancesport Championships, Alexandria, VA

2010 – Lekha & Giampiero Giannico, Holiday Dancesport Championships, Las Vegas, NV

2010 – Lekha & Giampiero Giannico, Manhattan Dancesport Championships, New York, NY

2013 – Lekha & Giampiero Giannico, Heritage Classic Dancesport Championship, Ashville, NC

2014 – Lekha & Giampiero Giannico, Emerald Ball Dancesport Championships, Los Angeles, CA

2015 – Lekha & Kostadin Bidjourov, Metropolitan Dancesport Championships, Long Branch, NJ

2015 – Lekha & Kostadin Bidjourov, Fred Astaire Dance Studio Showcase, Upper Montclair, NJ

2016 – Lekha & Jevgeni Davidov, Hudson Dance Studio Argentine Tango Showcase, Edgewater, NJ

2017 – Lekha & Kostadin Bidjourov, Cabaret Showdance, Fred Astaire Dance Studio, Cedar Grove, NJ

2017 – Lekha & Kostadin Bidjourov, Cabaret Showdance, Fred Astaire Dance Studio, Cedar Grove, NJ

2018 -- Lekha & Kostadin Bidjourov, Black Swan Showdance, Millennium Dancesport Championships, Orlando, FL

2019 – Lekha & Kostadin Bidjourov, Black Swan Showdance, Yuletide Ball Dancesport Championships, Rockville, MD

2019 – Lekha & Kostadin Bidjourov, Black Swan Showdance, Yuletide Dancesport Championships, Rockville, MD

2019 – Lekha & Kostadin Bidjourov, Yuletide Ball Dancesport Championships, Rockville, MD

2019 – Lekha & Kostadin Bidjourov, Yuletide Ball Dancesport Championships, Rockville, MD

2020 – Lekha & Kostadin Bidjourov, Black Swan Showdance, Fred Astaire Dance Studio, Cedar Grove, NJ

Made in the USA
Middletown, DE
23 December 2020